EVERY

RESCUED

DOG

HAS

A

TALE

Stories from the Dog Rescue Railroad

By

Deborah Eades

ISBN: 978-1-4303-1738-8

Dedicated to the memory of

Sam, Radar, Bubba,

Sasha, Gigi, Ginger,

Daisy, Arnie, Nicky,

Bruna, Biskit, and Pig

And all the homeless shelter dogs who never

found their forever home...

Their sweet souls wait for us across the

Rainbow Bridge

A portion of the proceeds of this book will be donated to DOGS DESERVE BETTER.ORG, a charity founded by Tammy Grimes and dedicated to getting dogs off chains and into the home.

Harlequin Haven Great Dane Rescue in Bethel, Ohio operated by Dale Bath will also receive a portion of every sale.

Photos in this book are courtesy of the dogs' new families, foster moms, and the author.

Every weekend, all over the country, dogs are being rescued from certain death in kill shelters and then driven by dedicated animal lovers to a new life in another state. Sometimes these dogs have already been adopted and just need a ride to get to their new home. Other times they have been accepted by a breed rescue or a no kill shelter until that perfect human sees them and gives them a second chance at life. None of this would be possible without the transporters - all volunteers who give up their day off and pay their own gas expense to save a life. Most would tell you that they are the ones who benefit the most, by seeing what a difference one person can make to a homeless animal.

Each one of those dogs who gets a second chance at life has a story about how he came to be in need, and the happy ending that came as a result of his journey across the miles. Since they cannot speak for themselves, I would like to share a few of their "tales" with you in the following pages, because after all, every rescued dog has a tale.

Fritz, Maggie, and Ginger

Our first adventure in dog transport started on a rainy Friday in February. Totally unprepared but enthusiastic, we took off for Louisville, Kentucky at 3:00 in the afternoon. Actually, we were to meet our dogs in Sulphur, Indiana which is just outside of Louisville. They were three homeless dogs coming from a kill shelter in Henderson, Kentucky where they were scheduled to be euthanized that very day before a rescue group, Avon Advocates for Dogs, from the Northeast agreed to take them. They were Fritz, a Samoyed, Maggie a Cocker and Ginger, a Cocker mix. Crates are used for transports for the safety of the animals and we did not have one, but we did bring extra collars and leashes since these dogs were coming from a rural shelter and had nothing. Towels, blankets, bottled water and bowls are also helpful but we were soon to learn about that.

When we met the dogs with their previous driver, Fritz was terrified and would not get out of her truck. Once we did get him out, he bolted underneath it and we had to literally drag the poor thing into our car. Maggie and Ginger were shaking but cooperative. Three more pitiful dogs I had never seen. My mother sat between Fritz and Ginger in the backseat and I had Maggie in the front with me. It was already getting dark and we had 2 hours of driving through Louisville's rush hour traffic ahead of us. Things we were not prepared for included the fact that Ginger was in heat and wanted to get up in the front to fight with Maggie, and Fritz got carsick. I felt very sorry for my mom as she tried to figure out why her backside was suddenly very warm. She then realized that Fritz had problems at both ends. Fritz took a long time to feel safe and comfortable with her, but once he did, he let her hold him and cuddle with him. He clearly was not used to human kindness but was slowly learning to enjoy it. We called ahead to my dad to let him know that my mom would be in urgent need of a hot bath and that her aroma was not very enjoyable.

When we met our next driver at 9:30 that night we let her know how upset Fritz was. She gave all the dogs a bath and helped them settle in for a good night's sleep. It would be their last night of homelessness, but their first night to know what a warm safe bed would feel like.

The happy ending to our first transport is that Fritz was adopted by a wonderful family in Connecticut. He now has a huge backyard to play in and two human sisters to love him. Maggie and Ginger also found forever homes. We realized that without the help of a rescue in the Northeast and volunteer drivers, these three dogs from Kentucky would have been included in the millions of dogs who are put to death every year in pounds around the country.

Fritz in his foster home

The Chocolate Chip Puppy Run

When the story of the "Chocolate Chip Puppies" was first posted on the internet, I just knew I had to be part of the transport to get them to safety. Everyone was clamoring to help to get them from Tennessee to an all breed rescue in Ontario, Canada. Their story began when a lady in Tennessee heard the sound of crying from the woods near her home. As she followed the pitiful pleas for help, she found three tiny chocolate lab puppies. The smallest weighed only two pounds and was later named Wink because he now had only one eye. All three tiny pups had been severely beaten, tortured, covered with paint and left for dead. There were two males and one female, with ears cut off, eyes gouged out and broken facial bones. She gathered them up and took them to her vet, feeling that he would recommend that they be put out of their misery. Instead he said that he believed they would recover from their physical injuries and be able to lead normal lives, but would need to be placed in special homes in order to heal from their emotional scars. Everyone knows it does not take much to kill a small puppy and whoever was responsible for this clearly had no intention of killing them but just wanted to torture them and make them suffer. They needed to find homes where they could learn to trust again.

A man with an all breed rescue in Canada would find special homes for them. The drivers were asked to provide extra cuddling and extra kisses on their journey, which was dubbed "the

Chocolate Chip Puppy Run" by the coordinator. It was divided into two days to make it easier on the puppies. My friend from work volunteered to keep them overnight at her house and I was to drive from Cincinnati to Lexington to pick them up and take them to her house. Her two preschoolers thought Christmas had come early when they saw three adorable puppies arrive that evening. My 23 year old daughter agreed to go with me to be the "cuddler" while I drove. She had never accompanied me before on a transport and soon discovered what I find so addictive about the feeling of being part of the effort to save the lives of innocent homeless animals.

In spite of all I had read about their condition and what they had endured, I was not quite prepared for the sight of the three small puppies. Tears welled up in both of us when we saw them - all wagging tails and puppy kisses even after being so abused by our "superior race". They were still willing to love us and trust us to keep them safe. No other species on earth has such a capacity to forgive and to love like a dog. It never ceases to amaze me the ability of humans to inflict pain on such innocent creatures.

My daughter and I had a really hard time letting the "chips" go when we got to my friend's home. We played with them and fed them and the kids were loving them until they fell asleep, totally exhausted. Being able to help them that Christmas weekend turned out to be the best present I could ask for.

The next day Wink, Leo, and Fortune arrived at the rescue in Canada, and their foster dad kept us informed of when they were adopted into loving families. He even sent us a picture of Wink with her new family. There were plans to get her eye repaired with the help of another lab rescue group paying the bill. All three are safe and warm and loved since being adopted by new families. Hopefully they have forgotten their horrendous beginnings. May they never know pain and suffering again.

Wink being consoled by Jessica

Hooch

We got involved in driving Hooch (who had no name when we met) when I saw an urgent plea on the internet for an emergency transport the next day. It was not to be a regular transport. They just needed someone to go to a very rural shelter in Southeast Ohio and pull the dog and drive him to Bethel, Ohio, about 100 miles away. This dog had been accepted by a Great Dane Rescue in Nashville and could hook up with a transport leaving Cincinnati the next morning. All he needed was a ride to Bethel.

Since it was a Friday, not a usual transport day, it was not easy to find someone on such short notice to drive that far. I was only working part time and had Fridays off, so after checking with my co-pilot (my mother) to see if she was willing, I emailed the rescuer that I could go and pick up the dog for her. I told her we could leave from Cincinnati at 1:00 and be there by 3:00 to get the dog. The shelter closed at 3:30 so we would have to make good time to get there, which did not seem to be a problem.

The woman who was coordinating this rescue called me in the evening to explain about the shelter. She was the head of a humane education group in Ohio trying to shut down the scores of county dog pounds in Ohio that did not meet humane standards in any way. They used barbaric methods to cruelly destroy the unwanted, homeless animals that they captured. There are laws already on the books in that state that describes the methods of humane euthanasia to be used so that the animal is not caused any additional suffering, but they were not being enforced by anyone in many rural counties. She began an organization to try to change all that and she was improving things for the homeless animals, one shelter at a time. She was now focused on getting this shelter to comply with the law. Her biggest problem was with the dog warden who seemed to not care for animals at all, and his method of destroying the dogs was to put them in a homemade gas chamber and pipe exhaust into it. Sometimes, many times, the dogs did not die quickly and they suffered horribly. He did not keep the pound open to the public for any length of time so the chances someone would come by to see them and adopt them was slight. On the day I was to drive out there, I was told to be there by 3:30 or I could not get the dog.

When we arrived at the pound to get the dogs I was shocked. It was no more than a concrete block building with no lights, no windows, only cages filled with filth and stench. The poor dogs saw us come in and immediately started barking wildly, hoping someone was there to save them. To be able to take only one literally broke our hearts. We knew what would become of the remaining dogs.

The animal control officer showed me to the cage where the big black Great Dane mix was and we tried to get him out. He resisted with all his might, probably thinking it was his turn for the gas box. We dragged him out to the office area to put a leash on him and sign the final papers releasing him to me. When we got to the lighted office, I saw the horrible condition he was in.

Underweight and covered in ticks that were the size of a quarter, he looked so sad and helpless. The officer would grab ticks off of him and then stomp them on the ground and blood would splatter. Being from the "big city", I had never seen ticks that size but she assured me that was normal in that area. They would feed on the poor strays so long that they grew very big. Eventually the animal becomes ill from the tick bite if he is not treated for them.

All three of us tried to load him into my Saturn for the trip to Bethel. Still not knowing he was about to be rescued, not gassed; he continued to resist our efforts to move him. At 105 pounds he had the clear advantage over three middle-aged women with bad backs and bad hearts. Since we did outnumber him, we finally loaded him into the backseat of the old car. We had put some blankets in the backseat for him to lie on. Once on the road, we thought he would settle in, but he was confused and paced back and forth. He would hang his head over the front seats as we drove. When we were covered in dog drool, we decided this dog would be christened "Hooch" from the Tom Hanks movie with the giant drooling Mastiff. Pacing and whining for several miles, we came to the conclusion that he might be asking for a bathroom break. Since we were sure we could not get him back in the car if we let him out to do his business, we ignored his whines. That proved to be a smelly mistake for soon he let loose on the back seat with all he had and he had quite a lot. It was everywhere and it really stank. We drove the rest of the way trying to hold our breath to no avail. Another lesson learned on the way to being good dog transporters -

when the dog says he's got to "go", you really should let him out of the car.

Later that day when we arrived at the Dane rescue in Bethel, we were greeted by a huge dog out in the front who was barking furiously at Hooch. We thought it was not a very gracious hello, but we misunderstood the dog language. All of a sudden Hooch jumped out of the car with more pep and enthusiasm than he had shown us all day, and ran over to the fence to see that dog. Wagging his tail for the first time and running back to us to say goodbye, he looked truly happy and calm. It was as if the Dane that lived there had told him in dog language "Don't be afraid. This is a safe place. They will take care of you here" We took a few pictures to remember him by, and then left him in the happy company of many other rescued dogs. He was given a flea bath and tick treatment and the next morning he was on his way to Nashville with the rest of the transport.

Our job was done and we were really happy for him. We smelled pretty bad, so before we could stop for dinner at a little restaurant in town, we put the soiled blankets in the trunk and tried to clean up a bit. We went into the restroom there and almost took a sink bath. All through dinner we were afraid the other diners could smell us. Out in the parking lot we were sure our car was all by itself in one area because it reeked and everyone else could smell it too.

The faces of the ones we had to leave behind would haunt us for many months. After that experience we continued to work with the humane education association to improve conditions there. Three months later, the county commissioners fired that dog warden, released the remaining animals to a neighboring county to adopt them out, and then closed that dog pound. It reopened the following year with a kind man as dog warden who worked with various dog rescues to get the dogs into a new home. We felt we had played a small part in that victory for the dogs.

Hooch was quickly adopted by a new family that already included a Newfoundland mix like him and they are quite happy together.

Hooch says Thanks

OREO

Oreo was the first pit bull I had ever met. His black and white face earned him his name, and he was as sweet as a cookie. I had heard all the horror stories about how vicious pit bulls can be, but since he was a rescued dog, I was sure that his temperament was just fine. The story of how he came to be on this journey from New Jersey to Lexington, Kentucky was another sad commentary on how far the human race will go to torture a defenseless animal and gain pleasure from the act.

Oreo had been the "bait" in an illegal pit-bull fighting ring in New Jersey and had suffered cuts and tears in his cute little body. Because his natural disposition was sweet and friendly, when the men could not get him to fight, they used him as the bait for the other more aggressive dogs. Lucky for him, the law came to his aid and saved him and he ended up in a shelter in New Jersey. Eventually, his picture and his story wound up on the internet with many offers to adopt him. His happy new family was so excited that he was finally on his way; they could hardly stand to wait for his arrival. I had the very last leg of the journey, from Dayton, Ohio down to Lexington, Kentucky. It was only about an hour's drive and later I would lament that I only had that short time to hold him.

My husband was the driver that day and when we met the transport in Dayton, he also seemed surprised at how friendly the "vicious" pit bull terrier seemed to be. Oreo jumped right out of the previous car and immediately started covering us in dog kisses.

I truly believe that dogs that have been rescued somehow know that they are being helped and give you their immediate love and trust. We got Oreo's toys and food and paperwork together and I got in the back seat with him so I could cuddle him as we drove. He lay down on the seat next to me, putting his head in my lap. I petted him and scratched his belly and he drifted off to sleep. Whenever I stopped he would immediately pop open one eye and look at me as if to ask "Why did you quit? Just keep on scratching!" So my hand got quite a workout and I was rewarded with sweet pit bull kisses. All too soon we arrived at the exit where his new family was anxiously awaiting his arrival. They could not believe the scars he still had from enduring the fight ring, but he greeted them the way that he had greeted every other new person he met - with love.

I kept in touch with Oreo and his new family and found out that he was sent to obedience school where he excelled, and then went on to be the couch potato that he deserved to be. Life had been tough enough already. Two years later they invited me down to their farm in Lexington to see how Oreo was doing. It was a wonderful chance to get to see how he had overcome his abusive beginnings and was living in a loving home. I think he even remembered me a little. I know I will never forget him.

Because of meeting Oreo and learning his story, I have become a champion for pit bulls everywhere and work against Breed Specific Legislation that is aimed at banning the ownership of pit bulls and other breeds that are deemed "vicious". Dogs are not born to fight, to maim, or to kill. That is a learned behavior and

Oreo never did learn it. I believe that pit bulls can be raised to be just as sweet and loving a family member as any golden retriever or labrador. Any dog will bite under certain circumstances, but pit bulls are just easier to train to fight with other dogs. All dogs need love to thrive and to be happy. Oreo finally got his and I believe that with more humane education programs maybe "pit bull" will lose its scary connotation someday and Breed Specific Legislation that bans them in certain cities will be a thing of the past.

OREO relaxing in the car

Shyla

Shyla started out named "Demon" and was a stray Husky hanging around the tobacco farm of a coworker when I was asked to see if I could find her a home. His German shepherd got her pregnant because he had not had the dog neutered, as is common practice among rural dog owners. He couldn't take care of the puppies and wanted to take her to the pound before she gave birth. I asked him to please not send her to the pound yet. The rural county pound would certainly euthanize her before she would have a chance to find a home. He agreed to wait a while so I could try to find someone to take her. It is hard enough to find a home for any stray but one that is pregnant would be a very tough order.

First I posted her story on the internet on a website at Yahoo Groups called "Dogs Needing People". Maybe there was someone out there who would find her story irresistible. I did not hold out a lot of hope but it was worth a try. I posted the story and waited. Less than 24 hours later, I got a response from a wonderful woman living in Knoxville. She said she had a sister living here in Cincinnati who would be coming to her house for Thanksgiving the next week. She could deliver the dog to her. Her family sounded perfect with two small children and a large fenced yard. They already had a Great Dane and were looking for a friend for him. This sounded much too good to be true. I went ahead and told the coworker I had a prospect for the dog. He absolutely could not believe I had arranged all that in less than 24 hours. I gave them each other's phone numbers and they were to work out the details.

The first glitch in the plan appeared when her sister could not drive the dog herself because she had a pickup truck. She did not want the dog to ride in the bed of the truck and there was no room in the cab. So she offered to drive up and get her in her minivan. We agreed to meet her halfway to make it easier on her for the 5 hour trip. It would be just like any other transport for my husband and me.

The following Saturday morning we drove to his farm and picked up the most beautiful full-bred Husky we had ever seen. She was being called Demon by his grandchildren since she resembled the dog in the current movie "SNOW DOGS". But she was an angel. She sat in the back seat with me for a while but then got anxious about leaving the only home she knew. She wanted to sit up front so we moved up to the passenger seat. Looking out the window with a sad look on her face, she almost seemed to be looking for someone out there. Clearly she had once been a family pet and we wished she could tell us how she came to be all alone in the world and pregnant. Why didn't her family have her spayed and put a collar on her with an ID? Her life could have been so different. Now she was about to start a brand new life with a more responsible family to love her.

She seemed to especially like men and the rest of the trip she slept with her head in my husband's lap while he drove. It was an uneventful drive and we arrived at the designated meeting place in Kentucky. She was very excited about getting out of the car. There was almost a tragic ending to our trip when I rolled down my window and she almost leapt out. I grabbed her and got just a bit of her collar and held on to her for dear life. We were right next to the expressway and she would have been hit and killed. I pulled her back in and waited until she was securely on a leash before we opened the car door.

A few minutes later her new mom pulled up with her two children in the van. They were so excited and the dog was excited to go to them. We took a few pictures for the scrapbook and off they went. My last image of her is her hanging over the back seat of the car seats and the kids hugging her. It was another happy ending except for the deer that ran into our car on the way home that night. The deer survived and our car was fine after the $5000 repair work.

But Demon's story was not quite over yet. Her new family named her Shyla and we kept in touch. My coworker was anxious to hear about the puppies and what they would look like. After she went to her first visit with the vet, I got an email saying that they had done an ultrasound which showed that the fetuses were not growing and two had already died. She had a uterine infection and they planned to spay her since the pregnancy would be difficult for her. It was scheduled to be done later when she was well. But before that happened she seemed to suffer a miscarriage and they found her lying on a blanket covered with blood and fluid. They were all sad about the puppies but were glad she felt better and was OK. Since it was almost Christmas they decided to wait until after the holidays to have her spayed. Imagine my surprise when I received the message on December 30 that the night before she delivered two puppies! She had not shown any signs of still being pregnant since the "miscarriage" She was even thinner than when they first adopted her. They heard her whining in the middle of the night and checked on her only to find her giving birth.

After a few months they found homes for both puppies, Tip and Tank, and they ended up living right next door to each other. The puppies are the spitting image of their father, a black German shepherd, with their mother's beautiful blue eyes.

SHYLA on her way to a family

Sophie and her Puppies

In 2003 I lived across the street from my sister in Virginia for almost a year. My husband had retired early from the police department and, since we were still reasonably young, we wanted to try living somewhere else besides Cincinnati just to see what it was like. We had visited southwest Virginia for 26 years after my sister and her family had been transferred there and we had always enjoyed the scenery and the climate. So with our children grown and taking care of the house back home, we moved to Salem. It was wonderful to be so close to my nieces and nephews, and my sister and I got to learn new things about each other's lives after being separated for so long. She had often said she wanted to see what it was like to go on a dog transport so we found the perfect one and signed up for it. We were living very close to I81 in Roanoke which is a main thoroughfare on the Dog Rescue Railroad. She had a minivan which I did not so she got to be the driver. Even better than that, it turned out that these dogs needed an overnight in our area and she even agreed to keep them for the night. And it was not just one dog...there were eight of them! We were scheduled to drive Sophie and her seven puppies that were coming from a foster home in Georgia and going to a rescue in Maine. Sophie was a rottweiler who had been found under a porch starving, emaciated and giving birth. Her puppies looked like black lab/rottie mixes that were very active and very cute.

It so happened that the weekend this was scheduled my sister had three grandchildren staying with her, so the puppies got plenty of attention. We partitioned off the kitchen with baby gates and put all the newspapers we could find on the floor. It was a beautiful April weekend and we closed all the gates to the large yard and just let them run! Sophie liked to sit in the shade under the trees and watch her babies play and tumble. The grandchildren rolled on the grass with the puppies crawling all over them. Everyone enjoyed playing host to Sophie and her babies. It was puppy pandemonium from 5:00 PM on Saturday until 7:00 AM on Sunday morning when we left for our meeting place on I81. Sophie was a wonderful mom. Every time we put out dry food for the dogs, all the puppies gobbled up all the food and Sophie backed away to let them eat.

For some reason Sophie became very attached to me and I had to bring pillows into the kitchen to sit on the floor with her while she slept with her head in my lap. Whenever I tried to get up to go into another room, she would stand at the gate and whine for me. So I would end up back in the kitchen holding her while her puppies played all around her until she fell asleep.

Our drive the next morning was uneventful. After clearing all the papers from my sister's kitchen floor, we packed all of the puppies into crates. Sophie sat in the front between us. She let me hug her all the way. This one was hard to let go. They arrived safely in Maine that night and all the puppies were adopted within a week. Sophie found a permanent home with the woman vet who arranged her rescue. I moved back home to Cincinnati a couple months later. But I will never forget Sophie and the wonderful weekend my sister and I had sharing puppy love.

Sophie and her puppies

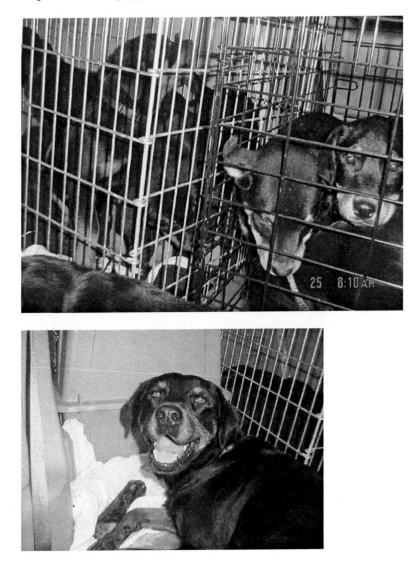

Dusty

As much as I love dogs, all dogs, I have an intense fear of German shepherds. They know it and they use it against me, I am sure. I have been bitten by a dog three times in my life and two of them were German shepherds. I was too young to remember the first one. Dogs can sense when you are afraid of them. So in order to be the very best transporter I could be, I resolved to conquer my fear. When I saw a transport from New York to Chattanooga for Dusty, a German shepherd, my husband and I volunteered for it. He could drive while I worked out my issues with the dog of German heritage.

It was Labor Day weekend and traffic would be heavy. Usually it is harder to get volunteers on the holiday weekends but this transport filled up fast. He had been given up for adoption by his mom, a woman who was living in an abusive situation. She did not have the courage to leave herself, but she wanted Dusty to be safe. Many times when there is domestic violence, the family pet is also a victim of the abuse. Recently the state of Maine was the first to pass a law that also protects the pets in the home when a protective order is issued, and now a few other states are following their lead.

I had no idea what Dusty had been through in his previous home but he was certainly timid. The first thing I noticed when I met him was that the "dinging" noise that my digital camera made frightened him. I always take lots of pictures of my transport dogs to put in an album to remember them. I could not take too many photos of Dusty without scaring him. I got in the backseat and sat next to him for the 100 mile trip. It was very close quarters for someone afraid of this breed of dog, but Dusty was very quiet and just as unsure of me. Soon he settled down on the blankets I brought him and fell asleep. He was a beautiful dog with one blue eye and one brown eye and coloring more resembling a Husky.

By the time we got to Lexington, I had conquered my fear, at least for a while. Dusty spent the night with a driver in Kentucky and on Labor Day he met his new dad. Dusty had been adopted by a wonderful man in Tennessee. They had hamburgers together at a picnic table in a park and bonded immediately. The pictures we received of them together would make his previous mom very happy. She had found him a happy home, and I hope someday she finds the same for herself.

DUSTY SEEKING SAFETY

Amie, JoJo, and Nicky

Of all the dogs I've driven over the past several years, there were never any dogs that I wanted to help get to a new home less than these three little Maltese dogs. They already had the best home they could ask for and they were loved beyond words. But the reality of life for working class families today is that many families are just a couple of paychecks away from losing everything. In order just to survive with a roof over your head, you have to give up the luxuries. The woman who took wonderful care of these dogs for 13 years lost her job, then her house, and now would have to live in an apartment where dogs were not allowed. She had no choice but to give them up. Her vet who had cared for them all those years had suggested putting them down since they were too old to be adopted. Amy was 8 years old and healthy, but Nicky was 13, and JoJo was 12 with diabetes requiring daily insulin injections and special diets. What chance did they have of finding new owners?

But the vet was wrong. Maltese rescue in Chattanooga, TN agreed to take them in and put them in foster care and try to find new homes. They did not have to be put to sleep or even go to a shelter. The trip for them to get to the rescue in Tennessee started in Pottstown, PA and I signed up to drive them from Lexington, VA to Roanoke with my sister who had a minivan. They were so cute and very much attached to each other. It was just heartbreaking thinking they were leaving their happy home after 13 years. But it turned out we only had two dogs to drive to

Roanoke because the woman who drove the second leg of the transport got permission from the owner and the rescue to ADOPT Nicky! She just fell in love with him and he went home with her. Since she lived close to his original owner it was a good solution. It was one down and two to go to get to Chattanooga.

They came with many supplies, toys, medications and a dog bed. We put the bed in the back seat and Amie curled up in it and looked sadly out the window at the cars and scenery rushing by. For most of the trip Jojo just smiled and sat up in the front with my sister who was driving. He seemed to be taking it all in stride even if Amie was very sad in the backseat. Eventually he got in the back and curled up with her in the little dog bed. They traveled very well on their trip together. It was hard to let them go and know what they had lost and how uncertain the future was. Being the mom of two dogs myself, I could not imagine the emptiness their mom was feeling that first night without them.

I took 36 pictures of them on their trip with me and I emailed her and asked if she would like to have the prints to remember them. She gave me her new address and we kept in touch for a while. Soon we learned that they both were adopted, with JoJo going to a vet tech who knew how to handle his diabetes. Amie has a new mom who loves her as much as her first one did.

I hope their previous mom is at peace with her loss and is back on her feet financially so she can once again enjoy the love of a dog. It is a true luxury of life.

Amie and JoJo missing their mom

Maddie and Her Puppies

What kind of an "animal" - and I mean "sick human"- does it take to throw a pregnant dog out of a car on a busy expressway? I have to believe they will face a higher authority someday for such atrocities. But that is the beginning of the story of Maddie and her two puppies that I drove from Cincinnati to Wilmington, Ohio. She was a beautiful Australian Cattle Dog found by an Animal Control Officer near Lexington, Kentucky by the side of I75. She had road rash and was in bad shape. The weather was freezing and he took her to the animal shelter where she gave birth to six puppies. By the time ACD rescue heard about her and went to the shelter to pull her, there were only two surviving puppies. They went to a foster home for the next three weeks to gain some strength and learn about the good side of humans. Even after what they had done to her, Maddie still loved humans and did not mind them being around her puppies, but she guarded them from other dogs.

A rescue in Maryland agreed to take them until they found permanent homes so a transport was set up. Cattle dogs have become one of my husband's favorite breeds to transport and they are so loveable. Maddie was extra sweet. She was up to about 35 pounds after three weeks of good food. The puppies were about four or five pounds and very adorable. When I met their foster family at our meeting place it was clear that Maddie knew they had saved her and her babies. She seemed to be smiling at them in the pictures I took and they hugged her an extra long time before saying goodbye. There were a lot of bittersweet tears, and their 2 year old hugging the puppies really wanted them to stay! I know he didn't understand why he only got to have them for a few weeks.

We started out on our journey with Maddie sitting with my mom but she seemed very anxious. So after a few minutes we pulled over and let her get in the crate with her puppies and they all seemed to be content for the rest of the trip. Although it was one of our more uneventful trips, it left a lasting impression on both me and my mom.

We later learned that all three of these special dogs found loving homes. They will probably never remember how they were once tossed out of a car like they were nothing more than trash. No living creature should ever be treated in that manner. Whoever did that to them will one day be judged for those actions.

Angela says goodbye to Maddie and puppy

Papa Bear and Benny

Chow chows are just about my favorite breed of dog, next to English Setters. They have a much undeserved reputation for being vicious, but they can be so sweet and loving and totally loyal to the human they decide to love. My husband and I had a red chow named Sasha for almost 12 years. When she passed away suddenly she left a giant hole in our hearts that may never heal. So when a transport coordinator called me on a Saturday afternoon to ask me to fill in as a driver for these two male chows, I was very happy to do it for her. We were to drive from Cincinnati to Indianapolis and I convinced my mom to help me since my husband was working. He had always wanted to drive a transport for Chow rescue and was so disappointed when he could not go with me. I prefer for him to go because he can do the driving and I get to hold the dogs and keep them entertained on the way. But on this trip it would be my mom who did the entertaining and refereeing when a fight would break out, as it sometimes does with two unaltered male dogs.

I met the previous driver in a mall parking lot and she had Papa Bear and Benny separated with one in the front and the other tethered in the rear car seat. She said they were no problem at all and I believed her since she had driven them all by herself from Lexington. I had brought a large crate just in case and I put Benny the black chow in the crate in back seat and then put Papa Bear in the front seat with me. He was the absolute identical twin to my Sasha and I couldn't stop staring at him. Sadly he just did not have the same sweet disposition as Sasha and I later found out he did not really like Benny at all.

After I picked up my mom we started on our way to Indianapolis on I74. When you are driving 70 mph it is hard to control two dogs who want to fight each other. Even though Benny was in a crate, Papa Bear was constantly trying to go over the front seat and get to him in the back seat. There was a great deal of growling and barking. That kind of dog behavior makes it very hard to drive safely, so I actually pulled over on the berm a couple of times to discipline Papa Bear. During a large portion of the trip he was standing with his paws on my mother's chest and we thought he was going to kiss her. Now if you are not familiar with the chow dogs, you don't really feel comfortable with a chow inches away from your face and staring at you. It made her quite nervous.

We learned from that trip that it is a good idea to crate dogs that do not like each other. My mother heartily agrees.

Papa Bear and Benny

Sam's Memorial Transport

When the first anniversary of losing my Sam was approaching I wanted to do something to honor his memory and keep my mind occupied so I would not spend the day grieving my loss. Sam was a dog I had rescued at age seven and lost four years later to cancer. He is my "heart dog" – the one pet you connect with like no other. He was so special to me that I know he is still with me while I help other homeless dogs in his memory. When I walked into the shelter that day in August 1997 and saw him lying in the pen with his back to the potential adopters walking by, it was obvious that he had given up hope. He was old and not real attractive and somehow knew the visitors would be choosing cute little puppies instead of him. His previous owner had given him up after six years so he felt truly abandoned. That forlorn attitude just broke my heart and I immediately asked to walk him. He was so excited and clung to my side and I knew I could not put him back in that pen. I adopted him on the spot and from that day forward he was my shadow and my best friend. If I left the room and he could not see me, he would actually wail. No one in my life was ever that happy to see me and now that he is gone I kind of miss the adoration. From adopting Sam I learned the value of "old dogs". It is so much easier to adopt a dog who doesn't chew your shoes or need to be housebroken. An older dog just lives to please you and he knows you are his second chance at love. I will never own another puppy. For me an older dog is the best fit.

So to keep me busy on that sad anniversary, I signed up to drive three, yes three, transports with my mom. My husband was in Florida visiting his sister so I was free to be gone all day with no questions asked. I was sure he would say I was taking on too much, as I am prone to do.

We started out in the rain to meet a driver in Florence, Kentucky with a male Brittany named Buddy. He was orange and white, about 8 months old and very energetic. Buddy was prone to jumping out of the car when the door opened so we had to be very careful to make sure he was secure on his leash. It poured rain all the way to Lexington but Buddy was pretty well behaved. We enjoyed his company and he was so excited to be on his way to his new forever home in South Carolina.

The second part of this trip was to be a crate full of four or maybe five English setter puppies coming from Knoxville, Tennessee. The mother dog was found starving to death and trying to nurse her babies. She was in a very high kill shelter in Tennessee when English setter rescue found her. They arranged a foster home for the mother in Virginia and the babies were to be cared for in Cincinnati until they were ready for adoption. They needed to be quarantined for a few weeks in case they had contagious diseases such as parvovirus or distemper.

They were adorable puppies and since they were in a crate we had no problems with them at all. We met their new foster mother at a gas station on the east side of Cincinnati. Since Sam was an English setter it just seemed right to help out English setter rescue that day.

It was late afternoon by now and we had most of our transport dogs delivered. The last one was named Honey Bunny and she was an 8 year old Chihuahua mix whose owner had recently died and left her all alone in the world. She was coming from Wake Forest, NC and going to a new foster home in Toledo, Ohio. Still raining and very dreary outside we got her to our meeting place in Sidney, Ohio with no problems. She was a very sad and subdued little dog. I hope she got adopted and lived out her remaining years in a loving home.

By the end of this drive we were totally exhausted and tired of driving in the rain. We wanted to eat dinner and just get home, but home was still hours away. We decided to try to find a motel and spend the night in Sidney. We could drive back in the morning after the rain was over. We called my dad to tell him we were staying and then looked for a motel. Well there happened to be a monster truck rally at the fairgrounds and all the motels were filled with motorcyclists. We didn't feel safe since we were two women all alone so we drove on to another town. It was almost 9:00 PM before we settled in. We had dinner at the Bob Evans restaurant across the street and then went to Walmart to buy pajamas and wine coolers.

We had a toast to Sam and all the dogs we drove that day in his memory, and knew that they were settled in for the night in warmth and safety. A new life was beginning for them because he had blessed my life.

In Memory of Sam

Forever in my heart

Buddy the Brittany

Karissa/Annie

Karissa was a beautiful 10 month old black lab mix found in an overnight deposit bin in Point Pleasant, West Virginia's dog pound. A dog trainer in San Diego, California somehow saw her story on the internet and just decided she had to have her. So she arranged to adopt her and have her flown to California where she would be trained to be a therapy dog.

Transporting homeless dogs from state to state is a logistical nightmare at times and when you add a commercial flight to the plan, it requires a lot of team work. A volunteer from the West Virginia shelter volunteered to drive Karissa to Jackson, Ohio, about a 40 minute trip. It is about two hours from my home in Cincinnati and my husband wanted to drive. We arranged a meeting place at a Pizza Hut in Jackson.. I was to bring Karissa back to Cincinnati where another volunteer would keep her overnight and then drive her to the airport the next morning to catch her flight to San Diego.

When I first saw Karissa I could not believe how scared she was. After we transferred her to my car, I sat in the backseat with her and wrapped her in blankets since she was shaking. We rode the whole two hours cuddled up together. By the time we got to Cincinnati to meet our overnight volunteer, she was getting a little more comfortable with us but was still one of the most frightened dogs I have ever transported.

Karissa made it safely to California the next day, and her new mom named her Annie. She says she just looks like an "Annie". She was checked out by the holistic vet and given a good bath at the dog wash in Ocean Beach. Like many Californians, she now eats a natural diet, and is very healthy and beautiful.

When I last heard from her new mom she told me that Annie now works with disabled dogs in San Diego. Her mom, Lauren, runs a special needs rescue for blind, deaf, and handicapped dogs. Some are missing limbs, others are blind or deaf. Annie welcomes them all and makes them feel comfortable and secure. Lauren says that Annie has taught fearful dogs how to play and enjoy life...she is her "ambassador of good puppy will".

That is worlds away from a dumpster in West Virginia.

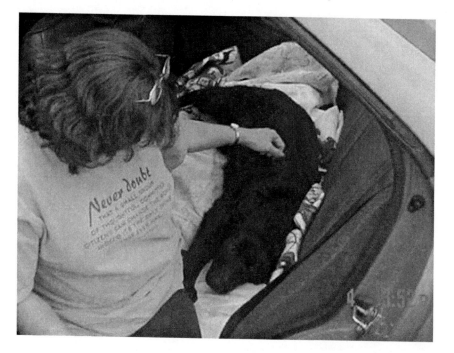

ANNIE HAPPY IN CALIFORNIA

FIVE CHIHUAHUA-PUGS

Butch, Scooby, Don Juan, Blondie and Roy

In order to be a responsible pet owner, spay and neuter is essential. If all dog owners did that one simple measure, the numbers of healthy, adoptable dogs that are needlessly put down each year would be so drastically reduced. Best Friends Animal Sanctuary in Kanab, Utah has an ongoing campaign called NO MORE HOMELESS PETS whose goal is to get all communities to have affordable low-cost spay and neuter services. So many people in rural areas simply do not have the money to pay for it, even if they realize how important it is. Besides cutting down on the pet-overpopulation it is also extends the life of the pet and keeps them healthier.

A couple in northern Ohio started out with one pug and one Chihuahua, male and female. After a few years of not being spayed the female gave birth to more than 30 puppies. The couple lived in a mobile home with all of the dogs and took quite good care of them in all other ways. But a few years later, they had a fire in their home, and the husband had to be hospitalized. The wife was unable to take care of all the dogs alone and was forced to give them up to a rescue group. She was lucky to be able to get them all into rescue instead of them being taken to a shelter and destroyed.

As a driver for Chihuahua rescue I volunteered to meet them near Lima, Ohio and then drive back down to Florence, Kentucky, about 20 miles south of Cincinnati. It was about a 250 mile round trip. They were all in crates and since they were so small, it really would not be too difficult to transport them. At the time I volunteered I was the only transport driver for the rescue group in Ohio so I had to drive a lot further than I usually do, but I did not mind. It was good weather and it was for a good cause. I took my mother with me and we would shop and eat lunch in Lima while we waited for the driver to meet us.

The woman who brought them from the rescue was so nice and she had brought her teenage son with her to help. We loaded the two crates into my car and my mother held Don Juan in her lap. They were all very sweet and loving dogs and had been well cared for except for the neutering issue. The one thing I was not prepared for was the awful high pitched, whining noise that Blondie was making sitting next to me in the front seat! She was not at all happy with the long car ride and she actually did serenade us the entire 125 miles home.

When we met up with Darrell and Roby from Chihuahua Rescue in Florence, Kentucky they transferred the little ones into their vehicle and we took a few pictures for the albums. After a few weeks, they were all placed in new and loving homes...and spayed and neutered.

My mom and I stopped at a restaurant on the way home to get some sandwiches. After pulling out of the drive thru we came across a golden retriever running in and out of traffic, closely missing being hit. Immediately we pulled into a driveway and jumped out of the car and tried to lure him back to the sidewalk with my mom's fish sandwich. He fell for it and we grabbed him by the collar as he devoured her sandwich. As soon as we captured him, his owner came running across the street, so thankful his only injury was a small laceration on this front paw from a passing car. It could have been tragic.

So all in all we saved six dogs that day and lost a fish sandwich. Not a bad day in our minds.

Blondie and Roy on way to rescue

SASHA, NEGLECTED AND STARVING

SASHA

"I was purchased in Florida as a puppy and brought back to Ohio. At first I was loved and treated quite well--I lived in the house as a family member. But then this winter I was tossed outside to live in a dog house! I even had a horrible chain put around my neck so that I would not get away. Then one day they stopped coming outside to feed me and all I had was my feces and mud to eat. Luckily then they called HHGDR to come for me as they did not want to get their car dirty by putting me in it.

Two wonderful women showed up to get me and they were so gentle with me, like I used to be treated. As soon as I arrived at the Rescue they cut the chain off my neck and gave me a warm dry bed inside for me to rest and even a bowl of food. I am a very sweet girl and just need a family to love me as I will love them.

As you can see from the 2nd picture I am no longer wearing the chain and I am much happier now!!

Unfortunately my heartworm test came back positive. I will not be available till I have received my treatment.

UPDATE: I have finished my heartworm treatment and am ready for adoption!! I can't wait to find a forever home that will love me as much as I will love them."

The preceding is an excerpt from Harlequin Haven Great Dane Rescue's website describing a beautiful black Great Dane named Sasha that was rescued from a neglectful owner in the winter of 2005.

They are the one local rescue I have worked with the most and they are located an hour east of Cincinnati. It is operated by a very caring woman who takes in as many abandoned dogs as she can with limited resources. Mostly she has Great Danes but I once took a friend of my mother's out to her rescue to adopt a little rat terrier she had taken in two years earlier. As a subscriber to her email list on Yahoo, I received an urgent plea for an emergency transport for a Great Dane in danger of starving to death near Cincinnati. Her owner had tied her outside (in February!), chained with a heavy chain to a rotting doghouse, and just decided to quit feeding her. He told the rescue to please come and get her before she starved to death. I was never sure if he just could not afford to feed her anymore or chose not to because he no longer cared about her. Either way she was in immediate danger and we had to go save her. After asking my best friend Kellie if she could help, we made plans to meet early the next morning after her kids left for school. She helps me so often that people we work with make fun of us and our "dog missions" It was a very cold dreary winter morning with a light rain falling when we set out. We had just a little trouble finding the house where the dog was waiting. Blankets covered the front windows of the small ranch house, and we heard another dog barking inside. Why would they keep one dog inside while letting another dog go hungry outside chained to a doghouse? I quit trying to figure out why people do horrible things to animals a long time ago. The important thing was this dog needed help and her time was running out. A man answered our knock on the front door and took us around to the bare backyard where he kept the poor dog. She looked apprehensive when she first saw us and showed no affection whatsoever for the man who no longer fed or cared for her. He unchained her from the doghouse and handed her over to us with not much to say. We led her to the car and she placidly climbed in and lay down on the blankets we brought for her. We could not believe how thin she was for a Great Dane. Her ribs were prominent and her eyes vacant. We started our hour and a half drive out to the rescue while she sat and stared out the windows at the cold rain. She didn't know it then but her life was about to improve 100 per cent. We were about an hour into the drive when we noticed that the tire chain still hanging around her neck was secured by a padlock. The man had failed to supply us with a key to unlock it so we were contemplating how to get it off of her. We called the owner of the rescue to tell her about the chain and she said she would have bolt cutters ready when we got there. It seems that sadly she has had to unlock many chains attached to dogs in her time.

When we finally pulled up to the property, the rain was letting up. As she emerged from the backseat of the car, we took some pictures of her for the adoption page of the rescue. It was later discovered she also was heartworm positive from being left outside without care.

She went through the treatment for the heartworms and came out of it fine. But now two years later she is still at the rescue waiting for a permanent home to love her forever. At least she is warm and fed and loved by everyone there. I wonder if her previous owner ever wonders how she is doing.

SAM'S COLLAR

After my sweet English Setter named Sam passed away in 2002, I kept his collar and tags with me in my car, hanging from the gear shift bar so I could always have a part of him with me. He was like my guardian angel when I was driving the homeless dogs to their new homes…I felt he watched over them.

Christmas week in 2006 I agreed to drive a Beagle mix named Sassy from the Adams County Ohio dog pound to Waverly, Ohio to catch a transport headed to New York where she would be taken into rescue and save her life. This was the only time I ever drove a transport alone but this dog would have no other chance to get out of that pound before they would have to gas them due to lack of space. So even though I had worked the previous evening until almost midnight, I arose at 7:00 in the morning and drove the 65 miles east to pick her up. I hate driving in the dark alone in the winter since I had collided with two separate deer in the past three years. My car is now considered a "deer magnet" and when I get new personalized license plates that may be my new one. But I put my fears aside for Sassy.

It took even longer than I remember to get there without a friend to pass the time. We had been to this pound several times to help save these poor rural dogs with not much hope of rescue. They need a good spay and neuter program in these remote areas if we are to conquer this problem of pet overpopulation. I arrived 10 minutes later than scheduled and I tried to call the next driver to tell her only to discover there is no cell phone service out that far. I hoped they would realize I would still be coming as soon as possible. When I got to the pound, the dog warden could not locate the vet's paperwork for Sassy and delayed me even longer. She had to have a rabies certificate to cross state lines and he never did find it but instead gave me a receipt from the vet's office stating it had been done. He just brought Sassy out to my car and dumped her in without a collar or a leash, making it very difficult for potty breaks for the transporters.

Luckily I always carry my "doggie emergency" items with me, including extra leashes. But this little dog sat in the front seat next me, just shaking horribly and afraid of what was coming. I felt so sorry for her that I decided she needed a real collar to go with her to her new life and she needed one that came with years of love and devotion already built in. I took Sam's collar from the console where it had hung for four and half years, removed his license tags, and put it around her little neck. It fit perfectly, and she looked so cute with it. She looked like someone cared for her. I petted her little head and told her it would bring her good karma and she would find the perfect home with it like Sam had found with us. I know he would be happy she was wearing it now.

I was starting 45 minutes late when we got on the road and with no cell phone service I was unable to notify anyone. The rest of the day would go better for the poor little puppy, I was hoping. When we arrived in Waverly, the next driver was waiting and totally understood the delay. She had called the dog pound and was told what time I left and notified everyone else down the line. After she got a little exercise and a bathroom break, Sassy settled into the next driver's car and curled up in the seat. She didn't seem as scared as she had earlier in the day, so maybe she realized she was on her way to a better life. As I watched them drive away, a little piece of my heart went with Sam's collar and Sassy, praying he would watch over her and bring her a long life filled with love.

SASSY

SIENNA

The first English setter I ever met was Sienna, named Cindy at the time I drove her on her way to her forever home in Pennsylvania. She started her life at the Morehead State University vet tech program in Kentucky, went to a Lab Rescue for some reason and then on to an ES rescue. She was seen on the internet and adopted by a wonderful family. I signed up for the first leg from Cincinnati to Columbus, Ohio one November morning in 2002.

There were actually two setters going on the same transport and they each had a large crate which meant I had to borrow a bigger car from my Dad to fit both of them as well as my best friend/copilot. We started out before daylight when I picked up one dog from a house way out in the country, up a long and winding drive with no lights. It was just a little spooky. When I got to the house all the lights were on and it was a hectic scene with many rescue dogs running around. The woman went to a crate in the back and brought out the dog we were to take and gave me all the paperwork for the new owners. I loaded the crate into my dad's car and set off to the next stop where I met with Cindy's foster mom.

Before I met these two dogs, I always assumed my dog Sam was a Brittany spaniel because that is what the shelter had told me. As soon as I saw Cindy I realized actually Sam was an English setter because Cindy was absolutely the spitting image of Sam, especially in the sweet, gentle eyes. I put her crate up front with me and with the door facing me so I could talk to her and see her as I drove. My friend and the other crate were in the backseat – a little crowded but it was just for a hundred miles or so.

It was absolutely eerie how identical she was to my Sam. It had only been 6 months since Sam passed away, but Cindy was born a month before Sam died so I couldn't chalk it up to reincarnation. But I just loved her sitting there looking at me while I drove and it gave me such a good feeling.

Now that I knew what breed it was that I loved so much I joined English setter rescue groups and try to help them get adopted as much as I can. They are so gentle and good with children, but they are very high energy. Actually that is why Sam ended up in a shelter at age 6 because his previous owner said "he wanted to walk too much"! I cannot believe there is any such thing as wanting to walk too much – it is great exercise for the dog and the human as well as beneficial for their health and bonding their relationship. Less than a year after I adopted Sam, I suffered a heart attack and walking with him was great for my rehab. He never let me slack.

Since I always take photos of the dogs I am driving to put in my own personal album, I had a few of Cindy to send along to Kris, her new mom in Pennsylvania. I shared with her the story of my Sam and how Cindy looked identical to him and how much I missed him. After she received them, she continued to correspond with me, and throughout the past four years she has sent me updates on Sienna's (Cindy's new name) happy life. She went to training classes and did excellent. "Walk" is her favorite word, like it was for Sam. She even has a trick she does where she can "bring a bone" when she is told to. She gets one of her Nylabones and drops it at Kris's feet so she can put peanut butter on it for Sienna. I feel happy to be a part of Sienna's happy ending, and to know how much she is loved. There are countless dogs and cats waiting for that opportunity to know love. They just need someone to help them.

I have driven many English setters since Cindy/Sienna but she remains my favorite. Someday I hope to adopt another sweet dog like Sienna and Sam.

CINDY/SIENNA

SIENNA IN HER NEW HOME

SIENNA AND KRIS

DO NOT TRY THIS ALONE
WITHOUT A CRATE

Transporting dogs is best done with a friend to help you with reading maps, answering your cell phone, and keeping the dogs under control so they do not interfere with your driving. If you have to go solo on a transport, it is a very good idea to have the dog crated for the reasons noted above. My friend Kellie, who single-handedly has tried to rescue every homeless dog in a rural shelter in Ohio, is a very good example of what can happen if you are driving two dogs uncrated who do not care for each other.

While returning from Jackson, Ohio to Cincinnati with two male dogs on a transport from West Virginia, she was headed for trouble. Moose was in the front seat and another male dog was in a crate in the back. She had a 2 hour drive she will never forget. First, Moose decided to relieve himself by lifting his leg on her steering wheel and dashboard as she was driving. She was lucky not to lose control of the car as the urine dripped into her lap. After dropping off the dogs, she had to go to work, and now her security guard uniform pants were urine soaked and smelly. With all this going on, she had not noticed her speedometer and how much she was exceeding the speed limit until the Ohio State Trooper was in her rear view mirror with blue lights. Luckily as she explained her situation and he could smell her problem, he sympathized with her. She just received a warning to slow down. Taking that opportunity to clean the front seat of the car and put a towel under Moose, she was on her way again.

Not five minutes later the dog in the crate behind her got the door open to his crate and tried to attack Moose in the front seat. As the dogs are growling and snarling at each other, trying to get over Kellie's head to bite each other, she is swerving all over the road trying not to get hurt. Somehow in the middle of this commotion, she gets the clip yanked out of her hair and begins weaving dangerously on the highway. She pulls the car over when she gets the chance and jumps out of the car.....blue lights AGAIN. A different trooper this time sees her as she jumps out of the car to escape the two fighting dogs. Then she hears him radio to his dispatcher that he is stopped to help "an Animal Control Officer with two dogs who are fighting in her car". He mistakes her security guard uniform for the county animal control officer uniform. This really worked in her favor and she did not correct him. He tethers Moose to the door handle in the front for her and then gets into the back seat with the other dog to secure the door latch on the crate so he cannot escape again. Once again on her way with no ticket, she is extremely grateful for the help. Eventually she delivered the dogs to their destination and hurried home to change her uniform pants just in time to start her work day.

So remember: two transporters or crated dogs.

Safety first.

HAPPY ENDINGS...NO TALES

The following pages contain pictures of a few of the hundreds of thousands of shelter dogs that have been rescued by volunteers on the Dog Rescue Railroad. They did not all have exciting or compelling stories to tell, but they all have one thing in common. They all got a second chance at life and love because someone like you got involved and helped them.

Look at their faces and see in their eyes the hope for a happy future and no more abuse or homelessness. Then go to your local shelter or to your own computer and check out websites such as Petfinder.com and adopt a homeless dog today.

Together we can all do a small thing with great love to make a difference.....

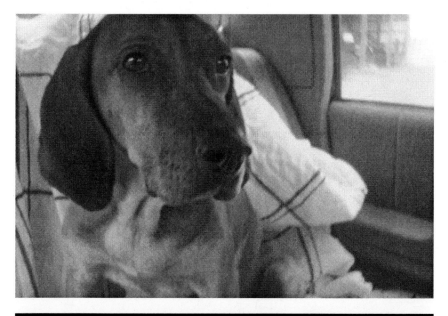

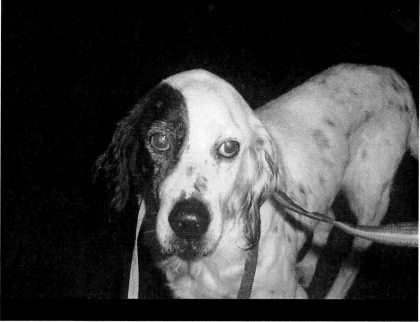

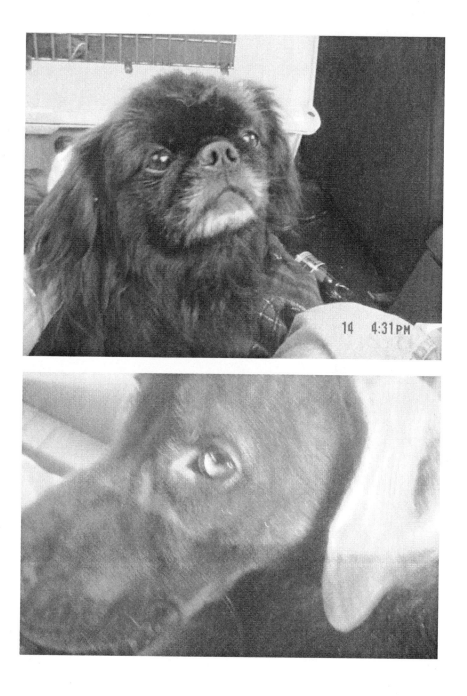

14   4:31PM

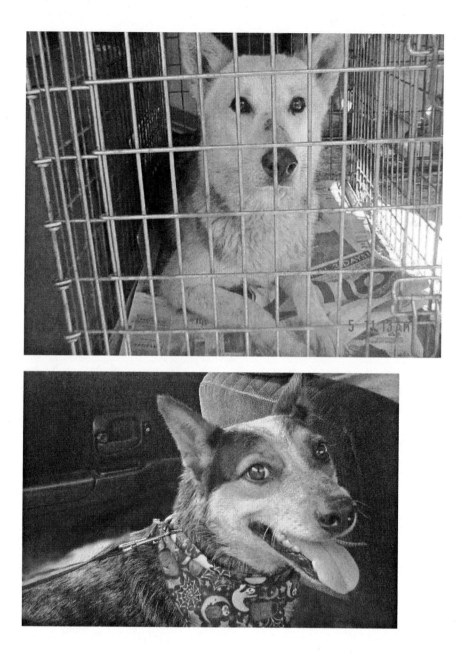

HOW TO

GET INVOLVED

.

I started transporting homeless dogs a few years ago after losing my dog Sam. When he passed away at age 11, I could not even imagine adopting another dog. There was no replacing Sam, plus I still had two other dogs in the family to care for in their golden years. But still I wanted to do something to help other dogs in Sam's memory.

The countless hours spent watching Animal Planet finally paid off one day when I saw a program about the Dog Rescue Railroad. It consists of animal lovers spending their weekends transporting homeless dogs and cats from animal shelters where they likely would be put to death, to the safety of a rescue or adoptive home in another state. Each volunteer drives a leg of the journey, anywhere from 50 to 100 miles, and then passes the animal off to the next driver until he reaches his destination. It is a wonderful way to make a difference in the life of a homeless animal and all it costs is a little time and gas money. There is nothing quite like that feeling of going to bed that night envisioning that homeless dog (or cat) sleeping in a warm bed and knowing human love and kindness maybe for the first time. It is the power of one person to make a difference when they find a cause to which they can dedicate themselves. There are thousands, maybe hundreds of thousands, of these volunteers across the country in every state.

You can easily connect with them on your computer through Yahoo Groups, MSN Groups, and other online communities. Just type in "dog rescue" or "dog transport" and you will see listings for transport groups that need drivers every weekend in your part of the country. The next step is to join the online group and email the transport coordinator with your information. She will need to know your name, phone numbers, car description and the part of the drive that you are willing to do. This information will be put in their database.

After you sign up for a transport in your area, you will receive emails and maybe phone calls from the person on each end that you are to meet. They will tell you what kind of car they are driving, their phone numbers and together you will decide on a meeting place. If one of you is running late or even a little early, you can call and let the other one know and also tell them if the animal is carsick or hard to control in the car.

This is a great way to meet other animal lovers and save lives. I have made many new friends in several other cities this way. There is a pit bull named Oreo that I even visited in Lexington, Kentucky two years after his adoption. His new family and I remained in touch. There is an English setter named Sienna in Pennsylvania who looks exactly like my beloved Sam. When I was driving her, it was like Sam was sitting in the seat staring at me. Almost every year I hear from her family during the holiday season.

When I first decided to embark on this new adventure, my mother wanted to go with me on the transports. It is a great help to have someone with you to help control the dogs if they are not crated. It is also safer if you are a woman in case of car trouble or breakdowns. Sometimes my husband goes with me now and he seems to really enjoy meeting the dogs and hearing their stories. My daughter helped me a couple of times, and once when I was really desperate, my 28 year old son accompanied me to Columbus, Ohio with two Dobermans. I really could not have handled those two by myself. Several of my co-workers have become transporters since I began telling stories and showing them photos of my "rescued" dogs. The fulfillment you get from helping these pitiful animals is priceless, and it is so easy to do.

PLEASE

SPAY

AND

NEUTER

ACKNOWLEDGEMENTS

First of all I need to acknowledge and thank my mother, Betty Daugherty, who gently nudged me frequently to please finish this project in her lifetime. Thanks to my Mom and Dad for letting me bring home stray cats when I was a little girl and passing on a love for all helpless animals.

To my friends and co-workers, Kellie Morgan and BJ Tomlinson, who have transported and rescued far more dogs in the few years that I have known them than I will ever do in my lifetime. Many times they have spent their last dollar on food and vet care for sick, abandoned animals and never hesitated to do so. They inspire me to keep doing more, until they all have a home.

To my husband of 34 years, Mike, who is the practical one in the house and keeps me grounded, yet always encourages my good intentions. If not for him, I would have been arrested for animal hoarding long ago, at the very least. I also thank him for driving many of the transports so I could sit and cuddle with the dogs and comfort them when they needed it.

To my children, Vince and Jessie, who always make me smile for being so proud of the responsible, caring adults they have become. Now they are continuing the family tradition of saving strays and working to stop animal cruelty whenever they see it. And finally, to my sister, my best friend, Ronda, who always gave me the confidence to write this book and never give up.

ABOUT THE AUTHOR

Debbie Eades lives in Cincinnati, Ohio with her husband of 34 years and two rescued dogs – Wookie and Snugglebug.

She is a member of many dog transport groups on the internet. When she is not in a car with dogs, she works part time as a registration clerk in a hospital emergency room.

She hopes the proceeds of this book will help fund various animal rescue groups and no-kill shelters across the country, and that many of those who read these stories will also volunteer with a dog transport group to save even more lives.